An Exceptional View of Life

The Easter Seal Story
Written & Illustrated
by Handicapped Children

Originated and Directed
by Edward J. McGrath, Jr.

Edited by Bob Krauss

An Island Heritage Book

Produced and published by
Island Heritage Limited
Norfolk Island Office
'Leeside' Taylors Road
Norfolk Island 2899
Australia

Please address orders and editorial
correspondence to our United States office:
Island Heritage Limited
324 Kamani Street
Honolulu, Hawaii 96813
Phone: (808) 533-4211
Cable: HAWAIIBOOK
Telex: Heritage 634206

Library of Congress Catalog Number 77-73684
This edition first published in Japan
Printed and bound in Hong Kong under the
direction of Mandarin Publishers Ltd.

TECHNICAL CREDITS

This book is wholly typeset on the
AM COMP/SET™ 500 in Souvenir.

The Nikkormat camera system and the
Zenza Bronica ETR were used extensively for
high-resolution copying work in preparing this
book for publication.

ISBN 0-89610-021-9

FOREWORD

In this book, only the words on this page are written by adults. All other words and pictures in the book come from the minds and hearts of exceptional children.

We use the word "exceptional" with a purpose. The "normal" child acquires effortlessly, almost miraculously, the gifts of cognitive thought and speech. With these come fully developed visual, auditory, and motor skills. But suppose a child does not receive these natural gifts in full measure?

Suppose, instead of a stutter, Churchill as a child had a disability that denied him intelligible speech? Presume that Einstein's brain had lacked a single wire on the starter motor of cognition, preventing his mind from ever embarking on the long voyage into the frontiers of science. What if Michelangelo had been struck blind at the age of two instead of seventy-two?

A child who responds to such handicaps, who strives to overcome such disabilities, then becomes truly exceptional. Halting steps, achieved after long, tedious, and even painful therapy, are more amazing, more breathtaking, *more exceptional* than the leap of Nureyev. But there is more to it than that.

The children who contributed to this book, like Churchill and Einstein and Michelangelo, each has his own measure of exceptional talent. In this book that lusty, living talent shines through the handicaps to reveal a unique and special view of the world. To read this book is to better understand handicapped people.

Again, it is more than that. To read this book is to enrich your own life with a fresh and enlarged view of human potential. You will find that the children who created this book are not only different from yourself, but very much the same. It is a most rewarding discovery.

CONTRIBUTING ARTISTS AND WRITERS

Ronald Lance Aho
Donna Albers
Evangelina Amaya
Shirley Anderson
Judy Arbec
June P. Arbec
John Archer
Devlon Todd Armstrong
Mark Barnes
Maria Barron
Leyla Baydar
Torrance Bell
Richard Blankenburg
J'meme G. Boyd

Napoleon Bridges
Marvel Broughton
Jimmy Burke
Mary Ida Burns
Virginia Fujie Butsumyo
Robert J. Carter
Edgar Lee Chandler
April Cunningham
Jerry Davila
Janie Davis
Linda Davis
Milton Davis
Mike Dollens
Stephen Doral

Shelley Irwin
Garnette Yvonne Johnson
Duncan Kearney
Robert Kelly
Danny Kochmur
Mark Koranda
Carlos Licea
Sandra Lie
Michael S. Long
Jean Martin
John McGaughey
John Mintz
Kenneth Mondfrans
Latosha Mosley
Marcy Mullin
Lana Murry
Jerry Robert Olds

Shelly Ervin
Henry David Foster
Boyd Fudge
Tita Galvan
Gerry Gladhill
Octavio N. Gloria
Jeffrey M. Gross
Gary Hampton
Luwona Harrison
Amalie Hazelton
Thomas Michael Hernandez
Denise Hiraoka
Morgan Hunt
Susan Ireton

Daniel Evan Opheim
Danny Opigin
Cathy Panelli
Erica Parham
Kristina B. Pearson
Rebecca Portnel
Joshua Schreiber
Gregory Paul Shipman
Kurt Richard Siegel
Chris Snyder
Scott Van Soye

Jennifer Lea Strack
Aura Strom
Bob Stronks
Arthur Lee Thomas
Howard Thomas
Zachary Scott Uribe
Carmen Velez
Joshua Vendig
Fred Vescial
Sallie J. Wesley
Darlene Wheeler
Scott Colby White
Chandy Whitlow
Veria Williams
Latroy Wilson

OTHER PEOPLE

I don't think anybody's ugly. I think that something ugly always has something beautiful in it. I don't judge a person of ugliness and prettiness in their faces, in their figure. I don't judge a person like that. I judge a person by talent, by their personality, how they think about other people. A beautiful person smiles

What I like about Easter Seals is they take us places, like shopping or to watch the sailboats. Mostly, they want you to go out by yourself. I appreciate people that try to help me. But sometimes they want to help too much. Mostly, I can do everything for myself.

Going downstairs, for instance. Some people try to carry me all the way. But I can do that mostly by myself unless it's too high. People that know me and are around me often, they know what I could do and can't do for myself. But people that I'm just getting to know, they want to treat me different so I try to tell them. I try to explain what they could do for me, what I appreciate. For example, if I'm getting to know somebody and the ice cream truck comes, they go "I'll buy it for you." I try to explain, "That's okay, I could do that."

The way I was raised was to do things for myself. My mother is a very strict woman. I got polio when I was four-and-one-half. She always taught me to do all I could for myself and not to depend on everyone else. It makes me feel useless when people think I can't do nothing myself. I don't like them to treat me nice, or any special way. I like them to treat me like any other kid running around—just like a regular kid.

People stare at me a lot and wonder why that happened to that certain person. I ask myself that a lot sometimes, too. God wanted me to be like this, I guess. I'm different than they are and they don't know why, so they stare at me and wonder why. They're glad it didn't happen to their children. When the kids stare at me, the mothers push them away but the kids keep looking at me. I don't like it when I fall. I've fallen at school and they crowd around and stare at me. That makes me want to crawl away and hide someplace.

There are always those who don't like you. I have a few of those, too. I guess, being in a wheelchair, people tease me. They don't think I can do something about it. But I do. I get pretty mad. One time I was with my friend and a kid came up and started making fun of him. I started chasing after him. I tried to run him down with my wheelchair. People do it just for the fun of it. When I was small, I didn't care. But now that I'm big, I care.

Sometimes people ask how it happened. To people who want to know about me, if they want to be friends, I don't mind telling them. But if somebody comes up to me on the street, I do mind telling them.

It really makes me mad when people say, "Okay," when they don't understand what I said because it's hard for me to talk. So I ask what I said. When they can't tell me, I get really mad. I tell them not to say, "Okay," anymore. I like when I'm talking to somebody and they can't understand me and they ask what I said. Then I'm happy to repeat myself.

I saw a movie the other day about a lady with no arms and she did everything with her feet. I was really amazed. But I think that everybody could do that, use any good part of their body. I think that handicapped people can find what they can do if they don't give up. I don't think that anybody ought to give up. If I try to do something and people say, "Oh, you can't do that," it makes me feel sad because I know I can do it. I don't want anybody to tell me that.

I use my head or my mouth or my feet. If I have a book, I turn the pages with my chin. I type with my head. If I drop something on the floor, I pick it up with my feet. I have a niece about one year old. When she was a baby, I fed her with my mouth. I put the spoon in my mouth. I make cookies with my mouth. I mix food up with my mouth and I do a lot with my mouth.

My mom never waits on me hand and foot. She lets me do it alone because, when she was ten, she had polio and she knows that I cannot always depend on her. I am very grateful.

I like to be around people. But I like to be by myself, too. Like when I get mad, or when I think of something really important. Friends are important to me because if you didn't have any friends, you wouldn't have anyone to talk to. Otherwise, I'd just be there talking to the wall. The reason I like them so much is not that they're like me. I just like them and they like me. We get together, talk, make jokes. Seeing all my relatives and my friends makes me happy. As soon as David gets better, we'll get together all night.

9

"I LIKE"

I like to horseback ride. When the horse is galloping, I can float away in my dreams.

I like to take my finger and paint mountains. They're easy to draw. I like to make closer mountains, and ones in the back more and more—like it's far away. You can put in the sun and clouds and the blue sky. They're pretty and nice.

I like it when you go out camping in the woods and you just have a tent. I like the woods and the animals. It's neat. You don't have the TV around. I'm not used to the quietness because we have ten people in our family. When I'm camping and I go off by myself, I think how pretty everything is and that it's just good to be alive.

I like camping out because you get all dirty and have lots of fun in the wilderness. You find rocks, kinds of bushes. If you go with your family, it seems that you have to do what they want you to do and you can't do what you want. It's more fun to go with your friends but it might be frustrating. The last time I was the only one in my tent. No one helped me. The other boys didn't want to sleep with me. I just went by myself. It was 25 degrees, freezing. My dad and Mr. Hicksenbach had to thaw out the coffee.

I like writing poems—making them up. It's a real neat feeling. I enjoy taking the time to think of them. Some are love poems, and some are just everyday, nice ones.

Robin

I first saw him from my window
Sitting out in the apple tree
His plumage so bright with colors
Singing his song of spring.
I opened my window so gentle
And tossed him some bits of food
Until he became quite friendly.
Each day, for weeks he returned
Filling my days with brightness
With his presence and cheery song.
Until one day I missed him
I waited but all in vain
Into the yard in search I ventured
Looking in the trees and on the lawn
Alas! I found robin
Laying dead upon the lawn.
As I knelt down beside him
My eyes filled with tears
And I knew without looking
Robin had been
The victim of a B-B gun.

Just Growing Old

The black fur is streaked with gray
But her eyes are still bright and shining
She stares at me with ancient wisdom
Even now majestic
Thinking of days gone by
When she was a mighty hunter
Still arrogant and proud
Not ready yet to lay and sleep
My cat—just growing old.

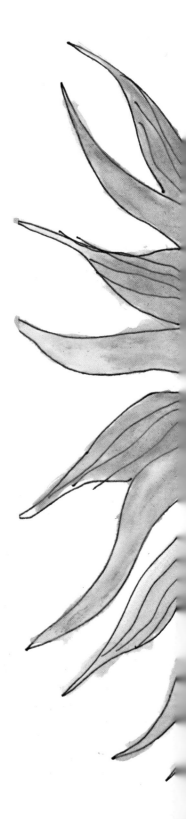

The sun is a pretty thing. I like how it shows, how it makes nice days. It makes things warm.

I like to look outside on rainy days—watching the raindrops fall—plop, plop, plop. Suddenly the plops go faster and faster. I get tired. The raindrops get slower and the last raindrop comes down. Then the clouds go away. I hate rain clouds to part. I feel the drops and plops.

The happiest thing in the world that I like— that I really want to be—I'd really like to be—is somebody who walks.

I like my brother. He is always tickling and telling jokes. Every time he does something so funny, it makes me happy, even though he outranks me in age. He's twenty-five and I'm only eight. When he's telling a whole bunch of jokes and I'm telling them back, it's feeling like I'm all filled up with laughter inside. He's got some goodies. I don't know where he gets 'em, but I'd sure like to find that place.

THE HOSPITAL

When I have to go into the hospital, that really makes me sad. I've gone in twenty-four times for operations. I go to the doctors every two or three months. That makes me all nervous. My first operation was three days after I was born. The reason I don't like it is being away from friends. You can't sleep in the hospital. I don't like the immobility in the hospital. That makes me the saddest when I go to the hospital.

It's the nurses and my parents, always coming in trying to beef my spirits up. They're like friends, the nurses. You don't see a whole lot of the doctors unless you need x-rays or something else.

Some nurses are not as friendly as others. Some are happy-go-lucky like the night crew. I have a good time with the night crew. They'll sit and talk to you for hours. They're more—to make you happy, I guess—to make you comfortable. They're fun to be with.

You get a lot of visitors in here. At one time, I had almost 60 people here. The first two days I was here my room was jammed. I didn't get to see half of the people. My family gives me a lot of support. They're there when I need them. No matter what time day or night, they're here.

There's not a whole lot you can do. I like to go outside, for the air. You don't realize how much you miss being in the fresh air, the sun, the cool, the flowers, the trees and everything. I was always active before I fell. I never knew I appreciated being outside, kind of free.

It hasn't changed my mental status. I'm gonna walk, right out of here. That's what's keeping me going.

HOW IT FEELS

A thing that used to bother me the most was being in a wheelchair. But after the fourth grade, that didn't bother me anymore. I would sit there at PE time and look at people playing tag or football and I'd say to myself, "Gee, I wish I could do that." I'd get to feeling sorry for myself.

Now that doesn't bother me anymore. I've gotten adjusted to sitting in this thing and I realize this has enabled me to do things that nobody else can do—to think more about things. There are advantages. For instance, being on the Easter Seal telethon. Nobody who can walk would be able to do what I did. Being on television showed me that acting is not all glamour. It's really hard work.

Afterwards, a lot of people said, "Hey, I saw you on TV," until I got sick of it. Everyone at school had seen me. My whole Spanish class quit work so they could see me. It was an exciting feeling to know that all those people were watching and listening to me.

When people say, "Why do you talk so slow," that makes me feel that I wish I could talk faster and be better and get rid of all this stuff left over from my accident so I can have a normal life like everyone.

It makes me feel bad when people interrupt me and finish my sentences because it makes me feel like people don't want to hear what I have to say. They think I'm retarded but I'm really not. I just talk a little slow from my accident. It messed up the part of my brain that does that. I just ignore it now because people have said it so many times.

One time I had a thought that Jesus came down with all the angels and healed everybody on the whole earth. I don't believe that will really happen. But I feel that everybody who is handicapped is doing a favor for God. If I'm going by on the sidewalk and they walk by with their problems, they look at me and they won't have anymore problems because they're better off than I am.

I don't think they are as lucky as I am because I try more. They can do anything just like that. But when I'm doing anything, I appreciate it more. They take it for granted. If anybody cooks dinner, they whip it up just like that. If I try to make a meal, it's hard for me. When I'm finished, I appreciate it more. Sometimes, I wish that all the people that are evil towards the handicapped could not walk for ten minutes, or talk right, and then they would see how hard it is.

24

It was a weird feeling when I first got sick. I couldn't do anything by myself. Everyone had to wait on me. I'd rather wait on somebody else. For a little while, I couldn't talk because of the tracheotomy. When I was in a wheelchair, I couldn't walk.

It's hard to get around in a wheelchair. It's hard for your friends to take you places. You tire easily. I think your friends accept you more when you're walking. They'd rather take you places walking than in a wheelchair. I found out who my true friends were.

I broke up with my boyfriend because we didn't get along after I got sick. I acted younger than I was—like in the fourth or fifth grade. A lot of my friends couldn't believe it was me. I lost all my hair and I was really thin. I cried one time when I looked into the mirror. It was really discouraging. I was wearing this ugly looking wig and glasses. When I saw how bad off I was, I started feeling sorry for myself. Then I looked around and saw people worse than me who would never get well again. I realized I shouldn't feel sorry for myself.

My parents helped me accept myself. They wouldn't let me put myself down. They wouldn't let me say I was ugly. I knew I wasn't pretty. But I was their daughter and, even in the condition I was in, I was pretty to them and that made me feel good inside.

Now it's much better. I can walk again. It makes you feel really good to be able to walk. You have to build up your muscles. You've accomplished a task that has taken a lot of work and exercise. It makes you feel normal. You're all excited to tell your friends that you can walk again.

Now I know why it happened. God wanted it to. It made me appreciate life more.

When I have a seizure and somebody sees it, they get scared and wonder what's up. Once when we went on a field trip, the bus left me off and a friend was taking me home. I had a seizure and had to lay down in the driveway. The lady was real scared. She jumped out of her car. She didn't know what to do. I don't want them to get worried, but there's no way I can stop them from worrying.

I'm happy that people care when they see me and try to help me. I love everybody that cares for me—my parents, my teacher, my doctor who is trying so hard to get me well. They have special feelings. In other words, they have love for me. People treat me very kindly, with respect. Sometimes when I'm in a park or something and they're fifty feet away and I'm going to have a seizure, I can't just walk over and tell them. It doesn't really bother me so much. I've done it so many times.

At first, it was hard to be around people that had handicaps. Now I realize they are no different from me. They are just walking with crutches and riding wheelchairs. A lot of people have handicaps you can't really see.

I flunked four years of spelling. I felt like I was nothing. So I tried again and I still couldn't do it. The teachers would back off and say, "Here, write this 10 or 20 times." It didn't help. I felt defeated. I began to get a complex. I gave up on it. I could write, but it wasn't spelled exactly right. It took someone time to figure out what I was trying to express.

Most of the kids were passing with A's and B's. It made me feel like, you know, when people leave you all alone. I couldn't express myself at all—through writing at all. In English and Math, if you can't spell, you flunk them. I knew the answers but I couldn't write them down.

When you don't learn fast, you're left behind to flounder on your own. You feel like they don't care about you. When you hit a low point with your friends—when you go out to play—you're picked last to be on the team. It feels like you're no good.

I blanked out a lot in spelling. When they knew I couldn't do it, I blanked out. It was more like a severe stomach ache. It made me feel bad, really bad. Most of the time, I was depressed in school. I looked upon myself as less than equal as a person. I knew I had a defect. It's reversed vision. A word turns around, d's are b's. It made it hard to read aloud. When we had history, I couldn't read aloud. I could read to myself but I knew I would screw up if I read aloud.

In the seventh and eighth grades, my teacher had the time. She put the desire back into Math and Reading. I felt I could do it so I tried. When I did it wrong, she explained the right way. I'm at the tenth grade now. I feel better. Now I can read a newspaper and understand it. Now I'm up in the clouds. I feel if I don't succeed, I can try again and do better than before. I'm learning it's not a child world, it's an adult world. It's neat to look back at the turnaround. I feel good about myself now. I feel I can accomplish something when I go out and try it.

FAMILY

I really love my dad and everything. He's a great guy. But he's sort of set in his ways. Dad has always treated everybody in the family, no matter if they're handicapped or not, like they're still his babies and he doesn't want them to go out into the world. I really love him a lot. But I just want to be independent.

Like what really made me mad was when my counselor called me into school and he wanted to know if I wanted to take driving lessons. I said, "Sure." I was really happy about that. All my friends drive. I've always wanted to drive. It seems fun. When I went home and told my parents, they said, "No, you can't do that because you're handicapped." That really made me sad.

There's two favorite places I like to go—to the store with my mom—and I like to go to picnics with her. There's two more favorite places. I like to go to my grandmother's with mom. I like to get out in the car with her. When I go shopping with her I get the happiest feeling in the world. I clean up the kitchen for her—play games with her. I answer the phone for her. She's not able to get around because she studies. It makes me feel fine everytime she asks me to do something. I do it. I just don't go off and do something else, I just do it.

She sets up the bathroom for me so I can take a bath. She puts on the TV when I get home. She sometimes cooks dinner, but I cook dinner most of the time. Sometimes I cook chili for her. Last night I cooked hot dogs and tater-tots, corn on the cob.

I feel like I love her very much. She thinks I'm a special daughter of hers.

ALL KIDS NEED LOVE

I think your parents and your family play an important part in how you feel about yourself. If they accept you, you can easily accept yourself more. It's good to know that somebody loves you and that they care about you. I think if someone cares about you, you want to help yourself more, get better. You feel like working towards your goals. It gives you a peaceful feeling inside. It's a warm feeling. It's important to have a good family— to have love for everybody. To love yourself. That's the most important thing, to love yourself and accept yourself for what you are. If you can do that, you can accept anybody else.

Some kids have never realized how it feels not to have any love at all. Some kids have never felt love and will never feel it. I know that all kids must have love or they will be different. I wonder what will happen to me. Will I become like them? I wish all people would love each other.

Things that make me sad is when something goes wrong, like in a family. Like when your parents are crying and you feel like you're in the middle. Sometimes I feel like I'm responsible, like I caused the trouble, and I don't know why. Mainly, when my stepfather and mother fight, that's when I feel like I'm in the middle. It doesn't have anything to do with cerebral palsy, though.

My favorite place is my room. All the things in it are my favorite things, my dolls and my animals and all my toys and my books. I like to be in my room when I want to be quiet or think. When I go it is all mine.

When my mom gets my check-up, then I can talk her into getting someplace. I like to go window shopping. My mom likes flowers. She knows how to grow them, but they only grow for me.

A NEED TO BE NEEDED

I feel good when people think I can't do something so I show them. At school, I work on the popcorn. I get it ready twenty minutes before. Then I sell it. I really feel good about that. In a report, I got a "good help." They really appreciated my help. They think I'm good about giving good change, giving the popcorn warm. I feel good about that.

But I don't feel good when I'm not good at something, when I'm terrible, and when they lie to me. They are trying to make me feel better. But if I'm not good, I wouldn't mind if they go ahead and tell me. I understand when · I'm not good at something. I wouldn't cry about it. I'd try to do something I could do better and do it real good so that special thing would recover everything that I did bad. When I do something good, that one thing takes care of everything I can't do.

It really helps me when they say, "You're not good at this, but you're great at that." That really makes me feel good, that I'm improving. My parents do that. They give me love. Trust they give me. They don't give me only things like presents. I have two brothers and a baby sister. They treat us all just like members of the family.

I know they trust me because, when my mom and dad goes out, they tell me to take care of the house, get the phone, answer the door, get the mail. My little sister is only two months. My mom and dad let me babysit. A lot of people think, "How can he babysit in an emergency?" I like it when they trust me. I go to the market sometimes with my dad to pay a bill or something. I go and buy stuff for him at the store. My parents don't think, "He can't walk so he can't do this." They don't think I'm different from others because I can't walk.

At home I used to didn't get to do anything. Once I asked my mother about helping her and she thought I might not be able to do it. I said, "Well, can I have a try at it." She gave me a chance to do it and I did it and she saw that it was good. Then she gave me the opportunity to keep on doing it.

I fold the clothes and remind her of things. She did a lot of things for me and I like to do things in return. Before, all I got to do was watch. I showed her I could even do it better than anyone else could. Well, not at first. Then, I got the hang of it, and I did it.

I like to clean the bathroom. On Saturdays, my sister used to do it and I didn't get to do nothing. I couldn't go to my room to watch TV until she was finished cleaning up. So I asked my sister if I could clean the bathroom.

At first, she kept refusing. I pleaded with her and begged her. Then she said, "Okay." I cleaned the bathtub, the toilet, the sink and the mirror. The only thing I didn't get to do was mop the floor because I might slip and fall down. That's how I got to help around the house.

It makes people feel good to help other people. Maybe you've been helped and you'd like to help somebody else because it gives you a good feeling inside. You like to see people happy and make them feel good. You like to help people because it makes them feel that somebody cares for them. It makes me feel good that I'm helping people. When I was in the hospital, some people had nobody to see them. I had lots of visitors. That's why I felt more burdened to visit those people who were all alone. They really need people to care for them. I know how they feel with nobody there.

When I moved here two years ago, I made a good friend. She's a woman seventy-two or seventy-three. She goes for a walk. I just got my electric wheelchair. When I went around the block I let her hold on the back of my wheelchair to help her walk. It makes me feel good. I avoid dips and puddles.

I'M WALKING!

"I'M DOING IT!"

When I was a kid, I didn't have too much friends. The other kids used to call me names like "Cripple" or "Ironside." Sometimes I got mad and started talking back. As I got older, I had more friends. Most were normal. There was a big park near where I used to live. We used to meet there every day. We'd go to ball games, concerts. They didn't treat me like the others. They treated me like I was one of them. They didn't care if I was in a chair.

A couple of times—I never thought I would have done it—I hitchhiked with them. It was kind of fun. I never thought I would have done it. I never even thought they would ask me to do it. Lucky the guy that stopped was in a pickup. They just lifted up my chair and put me in the back. When we were coming back, it was getting kind of late. We stood in the street. Somebody passed by we knew and he gave us a ride home. If he hadn't come along, they might have had to push me all the way.

I told my parents a couple of weeks later and they said, "What! You did that?" They said not to do it again because we might get in trouble. I said that was the only way to get there. I felt very happy because I said to myself I could do it. I could do it with my friends again if I wanted to. I did it maybe twice more.

Thinking I can do stuff by myself is a nice thought. If I ever go to college, I'd have to be able to take care of myself. It would be pretty funny for an eighteen-year-old boy not to be dressing himself still.

It took me five weeks, five days a week of practice at the hospital to learn to dress myself. My trip was at stake. I was going to fly to Michigan if I could do all this stuff by myself. The staff there encouraged me. They helped me. It took a lot of time. People had to keep me going. At one time I almost quit because I couldn't reach to my feet to put my pants on. Then it got easier as I practiced more.

Now I can dress myself. I have a bowel program. I can transfer myself to a bed and get up a hill on a wheelchair. I like to try things new myself. Opening a door is one of the things I'd like to try.

The one thing I think is that you should never give up hope on anything. If you want to write, but you think you can't, but later on you try, you might find that you wrote a bestseller. The doctor said I'd never walk, but now I'm walking on crutches. He had tried me on short wooden crutches. I couldn't do it. Then one day I was at the hospital and they asked me to see if I could walk on Canadian crutches. I said, "Oh no, not again." They're made out of metal and have a brace for the hand. I found I could walk with these whereas I couldn't with the thing digging in my arm. It was pretty exciting. "I'm doing it!" I felt like I'd done something that I wouldn't have been able to if I had given up.

SCHOOL

I'm in the tenth grade at school. I got straight A's the last five years. To get into the high school I'm going to, I really had to fight because they said they did not allow anyone in wheelchairs. One counselor said, "It's against our policy." Some of my classrooms are upstairs, all my Social Studies and English. I really had to fight them. Then I found out that another girl had gone there ten years ago. How she got upstairs was really neat. The football team—they made arrangements ahead of time—whenever she had classes upstairs they met and carried her up and down the stairs.

In the fourth grade I had the same fight. Then, I was on crutches. They said, "You can't go because somebody might knock you over and hurt you." They said, "Use a wheelchair." So I bought a wheelchair just to make them happy and never used it. This year it was just the opposite. They said they didn't allow wheelchairs. Finally I just showed up at the beginning of the year and they had to let me go.

This year I had six A's so I qualified for the honor roll. But they wouldn't let me on because they said I took four classes at home. But I got the same report card as all the other kids. Later, they apologized and they said next time they'd do something different.

I heard this one story about a girl who had cerebral palsy and she was in a restaurant. Somebody came up and asked, "Why are you in that wheelchair?" The girl turned around and said, "What wheelchair?" The lady got really mad. That's the way I feel. I know I'm in it but I don't consider myself handicapped. You are what your mind thinks you are.

I started going to a school for the handicapped. Now my school is just a regular school. My parents heard about mainstream and thought it would be better. Physically, the kids are different. Personality-wise, some of them are the same and some aren't.

My first year I became involved in student council. Even though I was a substitute member, I got to enough meetings to find out that the student council wasn't being run the way it should have been. So I decided to campaign for president. The way we have elections at our school is petitions are circulated. When a person turns in his petition before the deadline, that person is able to run for office.

I was thinking people would vote for me because I had crutches. Then I thought some might not vote for me because I had crutches. Some like me and some hate my guts. Maybe if I had a nice personality and I was in a wheelchair, they'd like me more. But I guess they elected me because they thought I'd do a good job.

I think regular school is better. My mom said that going to regular school makes you think how life is going to be. In real life, you'd have to get along with mostly people who aren't like you.

I go to a regular school, not a handicapped school. I don't mean to sound egotistic, but I don't like to be around people with my problem. I like to be around other kids because it makes me feel in place—normal, like other kids are. I like music. I play the guitar. I like baseball. I can play it if somebody holds me on the back. I swing. Usually, I have someone else run for me.

I think teachers care when they talk to you. They want you to have progress and be in regular classes. Sometimes it sounds like they're trying to get rid of you, but they're just trying to help you. Sometimes, other teachers feel sorry for you and everything. It gives the attention to me. When they feel sorry for me, they're easier. They say, "Poor Jennifer, we'll just let it go." But I guess if they keep feeling sorry for me, and letting it go by, it'll get worse and worse.

The advantages of going to school together is that the non-handicapped get along with the handicapped and that we learn from each other so that we're friends. They're just another friend. We play together and we talk to each other and we fight with each other. Even though we're different, we're all the same.

I wish I learned stuff quick. I've had some teachers that get mad and tell me I'm dumb. It really didn't bother me. Before, I was around people who hated school and always ditched. I ditched with them. I didn't care before I got ceramics class and Mrs. Mintz. I really like them. I don't have no reason to ditch now. I like school. It's fun.

I like every school I go to. There's not much difference, except that there's some kids with wheelchairs, crutches or braces, or some with nothing. But it's still not much difference. If I feel like running, I'll go to play with the ones that can run. If I want to just walk, I'll just go with the ones that just walk. If I want to play with them all, I just play something that everybody can play.

"TIME PASSES FAST"

I didn't win anything last year, but the year before that I won first place in throwing the frisbee. We went with the school team to the wheelchair games. It's for handicapped people to have fun. You can watch on TV. They do the javelin, the shotput. Each year they do it at a different place. I won the frisbee in distance and accuracy.

This year, they're going to put me in a higher bracket. I'm going to play table tennis. Because in school, once a year, they have field day—wheelchair dashes, basketball free throw, chess, checkers, wheelchair races. I came in second in table tennis. I really should have won. But I was overconfident and nervous, too, about being in front of all those people.

When I first started table tennis, I wasn't too good. I quit for a while. When I was in the ninth grade, at lunchtime in school, there was nothing to do. So I went and played. At first, I couldn't serve the ball. I can only use one hand. So at first, I couldn't serve. Now I hold the ball and the paddle in one hand and I can serve. I got better and better.

I feel great participating against other individuals because, before, I didn't do these things. I like sports. But I didn't think I could do it. The coach at school said at least try it. First he asked me if I wanted to go to the wheelchair games. You have to practice every day during your gym period. He's a nice guy. He likes to help people who are not sure of themselves—what they can do, what they can't do.

He taught me how to throw a frisbee, how to wheel a wheelchair better. I won second place in the slalom. You go through an obstacle course. You have to go forwards, or backwards, or around. You're working against the clock. I feel great participating because I didn't use to. I have fun, just enjoy.

When I surf, there's enjoyment. I get all excited. I get a weird feeling in my stomach. When there's not a lot of people, I can concentrate on what I'm doing, figure out what I'm doing wrong. I want to be good at everything I do. When you take off and get a good ride, people say, "Good ride." When you get a really good one, it's called hooting. Everybody screams and stuff. A lot of people watch you. I like the attention—a lot of people paying attention to me.

I'm a slow learner. I'm not too co-ordinated. I've been surfing for three years. People who have been surfing for that time do a lot better. But I enjoy it. Ceramics and writing are the same thing. People see it and I feel like I've done something good with my life besides just live it.

Time passes fast. I wish it would go slower. Sometimes when I'm writing at night and I get tired and I have to go to sleep, I forget what I wanted to say—my ideas.

I go shopping—to Sears with my mother. I like to go to movies and to the drive-in and to the gym. I like to go riding like when you go for a ride somewhere. Jazz music sounds good— real good. I don't like homework and going to bed early. I just like doing other things. When I go to bed early I miss a movie or something.

In football, I like O. J. and Bob Hayes. George Foreman—I like him too. He's a good fighter. Like Muhammed Ali. They know how to box real good.

What I like mostly is swimming. It's fun to get in the water. Since I learned to swim, I've won four trophies. I like to swim because it builds up my legs a lot. I swim at least two hours everytime I go there. When I first started swimming, I needed someone with me. After I got used to the water, I didn't need any help. They let me go around the pool by myself as soon as they saw I could take care of myself.

Last Saturday my boyfriend came over. I live in a house and he lives in the next house. He took me out on a date. He took me to the restaurant. Then we drove to a movie and a pizza. Then he walked me home. He's twelve. His name is Frank. He's good looking. I just like him. I'm nine. He takes care of me. When we go out on a date, instead of having a big person to take care of me, he takes care of me. When we go to the movie, if I fall out of the seat, he picks me up.

SEX AND SUNBURN

A couple of years ago at Easter Seal Camp, I met this girl. I think it was on Sunday. She has a power wheelchair like me. Her chair broke down and the camp people told her they couldn't fix it. Let me tell you, when that girl got the news, she started to cry. Well, I knew what she needed. I came up and asked her if she wanted company. She said, "No." Me, being a gentleman, I said, "Okay, I will come back." Ever since that day, until the session ended five days later, I always helped her if she needed anything. She liked that. The last night, she wanted to see me. She just threw her arms around me, declaring that she loved me. That shows you what happens if you go out of your way to help a person. I'm always that way—sometimes.

This is my first year at Camp Harmon and I sure enjoy it. I enjoy helping my counselors and, believe me, they need a lot of help. When I get older I want to be either a movie star or a counselor. I guess they are both similar.

In camp I go with my boyfriend, Vince. He's cute. We went to Formal Dinner Dance. I wore my pink dress and had four pieces of cake. He calls me his little butterball.

I like the pool. We swim every day. It was hot yesterday. I like to look sexy but I got sunburnt. I think I crack my counselors up.

My name is Duncan. I was placed in Cabin 8. The terror began that night. When Paul turned out the lights we began to yell and the terror began. The door swung open and suddenly Richard from Animal Farm came in with a pair of samurai swords. He started whacking the beds apart. He came to my bed. Of course, I wasn't frightened. I kicked the swords out of his hands. I picked them up and broke 'em over his head. He started crying and sucked his thumb. Then he chased me. I thought I'd better expose my true identity. My name is Duncan, the Bionic Man. I got out of my wheelchair and ran at him full force. Suddenly, my bionic arm fell off. I had to pick it up and glue it back on. It fell off again so I said, "Forget it. It's only two million dollars down the drain." Due to difficulties beyond our control this story will not be continued because the writer had to be taken to the funny farm.

In Camp Harmon I made a key chain and flower vase and I went swimming every day. I like the garden most. We planted flowers. Tom and I watered the garden and watered ourselves, too. I'm Esther Williams in a film called "That's Entertainment." I swam and they had water floating over my face. They had me hold the flag up with my face down in the water and kicking my feet. I dropped the flag when I dunked my head but it turned out good, anyway.

I love dates! We went on a double-date with Gary and John from Cabin 12 to the formal dinner and dance. Then we went to the water carnival Sunday and took lots of pictures. I love boys. I like campers and Camp Harmon. The rest of my life I hope to come back some day.

"WHEN I GROW UP"

I guess I'd like to do something for which I'd be remembered, like climb the highest mountain or going after a rare animal. The thing I'd like to do the most is something with a little bit of adventure to it—so after you got done, you'd really know you'd done something worth doing. Unfortunately, in my present condition, that's quite impossible. Still, I would like to do something that nobody else had done before, something that would be me at my best.

If the high schools are still built the way they are now, I'll have problems getting to the second floor. I want to go to college—like to University of Southern California. You have the beaches twenty minutes away—nice weather, no snow. If there was snow, I couldn't handle it.

I'd like to be a momma when I grow up so I could get my brother up in the morning for school. I could fix breakfast for him, lunch and take him to school.

I don't know what I want to do—maybe be a boxer. But I can't be because if I get hit hard in the head, I won't live no more.

If someone has a fire and they're in danger, so they call the fireman. I like those guys who play firemen. They can help you when there's a fire in your house. If my friend fell from the roof and I caught him, I'd be a hero. But I'd never catch him, he's so heavy.

I was going to be a fireman, but I'm afraid I might get hurt. You could die like that. So I want to be a truck driver.

If I could ever walk, the thing I'd like to be is a cop. I like to help people. I know I'd be an honest cop. I wouldn't be crooked or care how much money I got paid. Mostly, I'd want to be a cop to save lives.

If I couldn't be a cop, I'd like to be a lawyer to find out who's guilty and who's innocent. I would like it to be a full life. Even though I'm handicapped doesn't mean I can't lead a normal life. I know that I can.

When I grow up I want to climb an apple tree every day and pick the ripe apples and ride my motorcycle in the meadows.

I'm not going to get married. Me and my cousin are going to live together. Me and him are stick brothers—like stick together brothers. When my cousin and I live together, we might have his sister come to live with us to cook. Maybe not. There's a guy that's been here ten years, in and out of here. He's able to cook all his meals, so maybe we could do it, too.

"LAST NIGHT I DREAMED"

The night is cold and the sky is gray and I am
all alone.
In my soft white ears I hear the cold wind
calling to me, "Run wild, run free," it says.
I jump my stall and through the night air I fly.
My soft brown eyes see wonderous things.
I find my herd grazing and lead them on.
As I run with my herd following I hear the night
wind say, "Run wild, run free."

If I was a fire truck, or an ambulance, or a police car, I could go to a fire and have a siren.

I'm not old enough to play baseball or football. I'm not eight, yet. My mom told me when you start baseball, you aren't going to be able to run that fast because you had an operation. I told mom I wouldn't need to run that fast. When I play baseball, I'll just hit them out of the park. Then I'll be able to walk.

I'd like to be able to fly. Batman and Superman are my favorite heroes for now. It's not the amazing things they do. I'd just want to be able to move around. On some Superman episodes, they have girls who are blind and crippled, and he'll fly them around the world. I wish there really was someone like that.

A princess is pretty and beautiful. Last night I dreamed I was a princess. And I had a prince, and I was in a big castle with lots of people and I lived happily ever after.

SOME OF OUR CONTRIBUTORS . . .

Shirley Anderson is 16 years old. Cerebral palsy has left her unable to walk, with poor speech and no control of her limbs. She loves painting, pottery and swimming, and wants to be an artist when she grows up.

Evangelina Amaya is twelve. She has Pott's Disease, tuberculosis of the spine. She likes to watch TV and draw and wants to study karate.

Devlon Todd Armstrong is ten and has allergy treatments for asthma. He loves drawing and wants to become a paramedic.

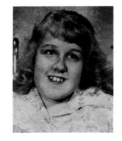

Maria K. Barron is 15 years old. She has a bone disease called osteochondrodystrophy, which affects the production of cartilage and is very painful. Maria has been in a wheelchair for the past four years, loves macrame, reading, writing poetry and stories. Maria would like to be a counselor and work with people.

Napoleon Bridges is 10 years old. Napoleon must have continuous physical therapy for his transverse myelitis, a condition which has left him partially paralyzed. He likes football, basketball, swimming and bicycle riding. He talks a lot about wanting to be a doctor so that he can help children the way he has been helped.

Marvel Broughton, age 17, has cerebral palsy which confines her to a wheelchair. She has some muscle spasms in her upper extremities and slight speech difficulties. She enjoys school and would like to become a lawyer or study politics.

Jimmy Burke is 7 years old. He had a condition (Legg Perthe) in which the blood supply to the hip socket was not adequate, and as a result the bone deteriorated. After an operation, he is doing well—walks with a limp which he should outgrow—has a great interest in sports, and desires to become a truck driver.

April Cunningham is 17 years old. She lost the use of her body and of her memory as a result of Reye's Syndrome. Intensive therapy has her walking and talking normally and her memory is coming back. She has three brothers and a younger sister, and since her illness, hopes to be able to work with handicapped or exceptional children.

Jerry Davila is 19 years old. With a post polio handicap he is interested in photography, ping-pong, football, baseball and boxing. He hopes to be an architect.

Mike Dollens is 15 years old. He does not walk because of the progressive disease, spinal muscular atrophy. Severe respiratory problems keep Mike on a respirator every night. He likes farms, animals, flowers and plants.

Boyd Fudge is 17 years old and has muscular dystrophy. He can feed himself, but needs assistance on many other every day needs. His interests are puzzles, models, flowers and gardens; and his goals are to drive a van, live alone and go to college.

Garnette Yvonne Johnson is eighteen and has cerebral palsy. Daily petit mal seizures do not keep her from being a very active young lady. She would love to work as a helper with small children in a nursery, or in a hospital setting. Her interests and hobbies are needlework and listening to recorded music.

Robert Kelly is 15 years old. Muscular dystrophy confines him to a wheelchair. He likes sports, reading, drawing, and making models. Most of all, he would like to become a computer programmer.

Mark Koranda, age 22, cannot speak or walk. He has been disabled since birth with cerebral palsy. His hobbies are business, TV, and movies.

Carlos Licea is twelve and had polio in both legs. With two brothers and a baby sister, Carlos likes reading, music and drawing, and hopes to be a teacher or a designer.

John Mintz is 11 years and 6 months old. John was hit by a truck when he was seven, and has poor motor coordination, poor speech and poor memory. Coming from "zero" right after the accident, John has grown into a very active, productive child. He likes stamps, coins, cats, camping and walking on the beach. The future? "Maybe a mailman, or a rabbi or a writer or a geologist—and so on . . . ."

Kenneth Mondfrans is 8½ years old. A bright young man, he finds his mild cerebral palsy very frustrating. Ken has two older brothers. He is into Citizens Band Radio (his handle is "Flying Dutchman"), AM/FM radio, music, insects, stamps, coins, everything collectable. For the future he has lots of varied interests—maybe becoming a councilman and mayor like his older brother.

Lana Murry is 13 years old and has six brothers and sisters. Lana was diagnosed as having cerebral palsy. As a result she has very weak muscles on her left side. She would like to be a piano or organ player.

Daniel Evan Opheim is 8 years old and is undergoing speech therapy, play therapy, and occupational therapy. Danny has two older brothers and loves to read and talk to people. What does he want to do when he grows up? Said Danny, "Everything!"

Cathy Panelli, aged nine, has amblyopia, a condition commonly called "lazy-eye" in which both eyes do not work together. She loves all sports, music, art, Camp Fire Girls, and playing with her friends. Last year she wanted to be a mother, this year it's a photographer.

Kristina B. Pearson is 11 years old and has congenital deafness. She is an ardent backpacker, swimmer and reader, and hopes someday to be a teacher or lab technician.

Kurt Richard Siegel is 15 years old and has intermittent recurring mild seizures which make balance and walking difficult or impossible from time to time. The seizures came from focal viral encephalitis. Kurt has a brother and sister, likes to work on mechanical things, has his own Go-cart and would like to become an auto or motorcycle mechanic.

Gregory Paul Shipman is 12½ years old. Affected by spastic cerebral palsy, the muscles in his arms and legs are not able to function normally. Gregory is headed toward becoming a disc jockey. He enjoys his favorite rock music, comic books and stamp collecting.

Jennifer Lea Strack is 15 and has a learning disability. Her interests are swimming, horseback riding, drawing, and writing. One day she plans to be an actress, singer or model.

Bob Stronks is 10 years old and has had ten major surgical operations since his injury in an automobile accident. With some speech disability he also has partial paralysis of his right arm and leg. He is an ardent cub scout, likes kites, bike riding, swimming, and his cat. The idea of someday becoming either a truck driver or a chef is his present goal.

Howard Thomas is ten and has muscular dystrophy. He loves his small car collection, stamps, and sports. Howard has an older brother and sister and someday wants to be a sports writer or announcer.

Scott Van Soye is 13 years old. Severely handicapped since birth with cerebral palsy Scott has struggled to learn to walk a few steps with crutches. He spends 99% of his time in a wheelchair. Reading and chess are his hobbies and he hopes to be an attorney-at-law.

Fred Vescial is twelve and has two younger brothers. He has had over twenty operations, is paraplegic with arrested hydrocephalus. His hobbies and interests include sports, guitar and travel, and he is pointing now toward being either a sportscaster or a lawyer.

Scott Colby White is 12 years old. Mild cerebral palsy has left him slow in school and less accepted by his peers than he would like to be. He has an older sister, loves working on bikes, reading logging books, and hasn't yet said what he wants to be when he grows up.

Chandy Whitlow is nine and is paralyzed from the waist down. She has no bowel or bladder control and has a shunt to drain fluid off her brain. An only child, Chandy loves TV, games, talking on the phone, music, and helping mom with her housework. She hopes to be either a secretary or a teacher.

Dyanne Y. McGrath
Associate Director
A Child's Point of View Library

Howard Jaroslovsky
Assistant Director
Compiler and Interviewer

Eleanor Marsee
Assistant Editor

Kenyon S. Chan, Ph.D., UCLA
Educational Consultant

We wish to thank the Easter Seal Society for Crippled Children and Adults of California, its Board of Directors, and its Executive Director. We also appreciate the help and cooperation of all the local Easter Seal Societies, their Executive Directors—and a great group of volunteers for helping to make possible this unique addition to A Child's Point of View Library.

The Publishers acknowledge the contributions of The Exceptional Children's Foundation through its art training program.

A special word of thanks to Pan American World Airways.

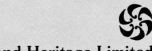

Island Heritage Limited

EDITORS
Robert B. Goodman
Robert A. Spicer

PRODUCTION EDITOR
Kitty D. Dabney

PRODUCTION SUPERVISOR
Janice Otaguro

PRODUCTION ASSISTANT
Nancy R. Clark

TYPOGRAPHY
Barbara Goodman
Diana Haskell